Reformation and Counter-Reformation

1588 - 1688 - 1988
by
J. R. Broome

GOSPEL STANDARD TRUST PUBLICATIONS

1988

7 Brackendale Grove, Harpenden,
Herts. AL5 3EL
England

© Gospel Standard Trust 1988

ISBN 0 903556 79 0

Typeset by
Millford Reprographics International Limited, Luton, Beds.

Printed and bound by
Whitstable Litho Printers Limited, Whitstable, Kent.

CONTENTS

		Page
Introduction		
1.	The Armada – 1588	1
2.	The Glorious Revolution – 1688	13
3.	Anglican-Roman Catholic Reunion – 1988	29

The front cover shows the spire of Salisbury Cathedral.

Introduction

1588 - 1688 - 1988. These years mark the three major attempts by the Roman Catholic Church to recover Britain for the Catholic Faith. The first attempt was an amphibious operation by the Spanish Armada, identical in conception to those of Napoleon and Hitler. Next was an attempt through a Roman Catholic monarch, James II to take over the Judiciary, Army and Administration and remove the Protestant Constitution of the Nation. The third attempt is to change the Anglican Church internally, and through the Anglican Roman Catholic International Commission, bring about a reconciliation and reunion of the Anglican Communion with the See of Rome.

Ever since the Reformation in the time of Luther, nearly 500 years ago, Rome has been working to recover the lost provinces of her Church. She is not to be underrated in her tenacity in holding to her "Faith". It is a faith which embodies much that is unscriptural, and her consistent aim is never to give up until all the nations of the world bow to her dominion. When the Pope lands from his aircraft with his Papal entourage on his various world tours, it is of prime importance to him that he kiss the soil of the country to which he has come. This is no idle gesture, but conveys to his followers his claims to sovereignty, as God's vicegerent on this earth, and announces the arrival and the sovereign claims of "the earthly agent of the King of Kings". His title is, "Prince of the Kings of the earth".

The aim of this book is to give a brief survey of these three attempts to change the Protestant constitution of this country, two of which are to be commemorated in 1988 for their failure, and one of which hangs in the balance in that year dependent upon the decisions of the Lambeth Conference in July/August 1988, and further discussions in the Church of England.

CHAPTER 1

The Armada – 1588

The English Reformation

Elizabeth I had been Queen for 29 years when Philip II of Spain organised his Great Enterprise to dethrone her. By 1588 Britain and Spain had been for some years in semi-open conflict over the command of the High Seas. Spain was already a great world power with extensive interests in North and South America. Spanish ships were stopped at sea by British privateers such as Francis Drake, and their treasures from the New World were pirated. But this was not the major cause of the Armada. The roots were far deeper. It was a religious crusade fully supported by the Papacy to restore the Roman Catholic Faith in Britain. The schism with Rome which had commenced for political purposes in the reign of Henry VIII had deepened in the reign of Edward VI under the leadership of Archbishop Cranmer with the introduction of the Second Prayer Book of 1552 which was a Protestant document. It had received a setback when "Bloody Mary" became Queen in 1553. During her reign for a period of three years from 4th February 1555 with the burning of John Rogers at Smithfield, there commenced, at a rate of 90 a year, a holocaust of burnings of innocent people who refused to accept the Catholic Faith. They included the Archbishop of Canterbury, Thomas Cranmer; the Bishop of Gloucester, John Hooper; the Bishop of London, Nicholas Ridley; the former Bishop of Worcester, Hugh Latimer; a Chaplain of Edward VI, John Bradford; 100 clergymen, 60 women, and many ordinary people. Most were burnt in the London area and the Home Counties, the strongest areas of Protestantism. Many educated and distinguished men and women went into exile to Germany and Switzerland where they stayed until the accession of Elizabeth I in 1558. The effect of this scourge of Protestantism was to increase its strength as the noble army of martyrs stood the test of their faith in the flames. Hugh Latimer in the flames outside Balliol College, Oxford on 16th October 1555 made his historic remark to his fellow sufferer Nicholas Ridley, "Be of good comfort Master Ridley, and play the man; we shall this day light a candle, by God's grace in England, as I trust shall never shall be put out". Archbishop Cranmer after five recantations of

1

the Reformed Faith, finally held the offending hand that had signed the recantations in the flames and watched it burn as he died at Oxford. Years before (6th October 1536) at Vilvorde in Belgium, William Tyndale, the translator of the Bible into English had died in the flames for his work. "Bloody Mary" was the daughter of Catherine of Aragon, a Spanish Princess, first wife of Henry VIII. Being half-Spanish and wanting to restore the Catholic Faith in Britain, she had married her cousin Philip II of Spain at Winchester Cathedral in 1554, just prior to the burnings. They had no family, nor was he allowed by Parliament to become King of England. The marriage was very unsuccessful and after 18 months, he returned to Spain. On her death in 1558, Mary was succeeded by her half-sister, Elizabeth, the daughter of Anne Boleyn, the wife which Henry VIII had had beheaded in 1536. Elizabeth favoured the Protestants mainly because she wanted to keep Britain as an independent country. Protestant exiles, like Edmund Grindal and John Jewel, were given prominent places by her in the Church of England and the Book of Common Prayer and the Thirty Nine Articles of the Church of England established the Protestant Faith in this country.

The Papal Bull(1570)

By February 1570 Pope Pius V had determined that Britain was beyond hope of immediate recovery and decided to issue a Bull, "Regnans in Excelsis", against the Throne and Constitution of Britain, excommunicating "the heretical, illegitimate" daughter of Henry VIII. The Bull entitled "The Damnation and Excommunication of Elizabeth, Queen of England and her adherents" declares, "He that reigneth on high, to whom is given all power in heaven and in earth, committed one Holy, Catholic and Apostolic Church (out of which there is no salvation) to one alone upon earth, namely to Peter, the Prince of the Apostles, and to Peter's successor the Bishop of Rome, to be governed in fullness of power. Him alone He made Prince over all people and all kingdoms, to pluck up, destroy, scatter, consume, plant, and build. We do, out of the fullness of our apostolic power, declare the aforesaid Elizabeth being a heretic, and a favourer of heretics, and her adherents in the manner aforesaid, to have incurred the sentence of anathema, and to be cut off from the unity of the body of Christ. And moreover, we do declare her to be deprived of her pretended title to the kingdom aforesaid, and all dominion, dignity, and privilege whatsoever. And also the nobility, subjects, and people of the said kingdom, and all others which have in any sort sworn to her, to be forever absolved from any such oath and all manner of duty, dominion, allegiance, and obedience; as we do by the authority of these presentments absolve them, and deprive the said Elizabeth of her pretended title to the kingdom and all other things above said. And we do command and interdict all and every, the noblemen, subjects, people and others aforesaid that they presume not to obey her or her admonitions, mandates, and laws. And those who shall act contrary we involve in the same sentence of anathema". The loyalty of Elizabeth's Catholic subjects was now seriously in question and she responded with laws against Catholics.

The Counter-Reformation

The Catholic Church had by this time taken a survey of the Reformation and a survey of their own position relative to it. In 1542, the Holy Office had been established in Rome, the Central Administration of the Inquisition, the vicious organisation aimed at the extermination of Protestants by torture. About the same time, in 1540, the Society of Jesus or the Jesuits had been established, whose principal function was to win back the Protestant countries of Europe by political means. Founded by Don Inigo Lopez De Loyola, (St. Ignatius) the Jesuit teachers and confessors worked among the nobility and royalty of Catholic Europe using methods akin to the Diplomatic Corps and the Secret Service. In 1545 the Council of Trent had met and continued intermittently until 1563. At this major Council of the Roman Catholic Church, a full statement of the Canons of the Church had been declared and their answer given to the Reformation. War was there and then declared upon Reformation Doctrines, and the Counter-Reformation was launched, and is very much still in progress. 1563 in fact, was the high water mark of Protestantism. Thereafter the Roman Catholic Church retained all in Europe that was left to it then, and has since made serious encroachments upon what the Reformation had taken from it. This extensive enterprise for the recovery of Protestant Europe to the Roman Catholic Faith depended on Spanish military and naval might, the armoury of Philip II of Spain, for its first major counter attacks. The wealth that came from America in the form of silver bullion was used to pay for them.

The Spanish Attack on the Netherlands

One such conflict was in the Spanish Netherlands. There the Government of Philip II had so embittered the Dutch, that in 1566 they had risen in rebellion. Initially the Duke of Alva was sent to suppress the rebellion and restore the Catholic Faith. William the Silent headed a group of noblemen to ask for various rights. The Spanish rejected these men as "Beggars" and they at once styled themselves "Sea Beggars", organised their own fleet and attacked the Spanish Ships in the Channel and North Sea. In 1578 Alexander Farnese, Duke of Parma, was sent with an army to the area to crush the rebellion, and had numerous successes. Then in 1584 "William the Silent, the most illustrious victim of that campaign of legalised murder by which the Counter-Reformation sought to eliminate its key opponents" (Tudor England. S.T.Bindoff. p. 264) was assassinated by Balthasar Gerard and the blood money was promptly paid to his relatives by Philip of Spain (William the Silent. C.V.Wedgwood. p.250).

St. Bartholomew's Day (1572)

Across the frontiers in France another bloodbath was going on. St. Bartholomew's Day, 24th August 1572 was the day when Admiral Coligny, leader of the Huguenot Protestants and 4,000 of his fellow Huguenots were massacred in the streets of Paris and their bodies thrown into the River Seine, to be followed by similar massacres throughout the towns of France. Who were the instigators of this crime is not easy to prove conclusively. Certainly the Royal Household of France had the major hand in it. At the news of the massacre Pope Gregory XIII ordered a solemn "Te Deum" to be sung, "Was duly delighted and had a special medal struck to commemorate the great event" (Europe Divided. J.H.Elliott. p.220); and "Philip of Spain burst into his only recorded laugh" (Europe. F.Schevill. p.206). It is hardly surprising that Protestants were fully persuaded that the event had been planned between France, Spain and Rome. It left a very solemn dread in the hearts of all Protestants in Europe, as coupled with the Fires of Smithfield and the macabre Spanish Inquisition, Protestants came under attack for their Faith in circumstances little different to Hitler's persecution of the Jews.

The Counter-Reformation in England

In England, Elizabeth and her Government were under threat from activists, within and without, of the Counter-Reformation. The introduction of the Papal Bull of 1570 and the things which the document encouraged English Catholics to do, were declared treason. In 1568, William Allen, formerly Principal of an Oxford College had established an English College at Douai in the Spanish Netherlands, its primary purpose to train Catholic missionaries for England. Later it moved to Rheims and in 1579 another College was founded in Rome. The first Catholic missionaries arrived in England in 1574 and by 1580 there were over 100 secretly moving around the country, "Breathing into English Catholicism something of the restless vitality of the Counter-Reformation" (Tudor England. S.T.Bindoff. p.236). "Seen as individuals these missionaries were true heroes and martyrs yet the fact remains that they were sent by their superiors and rulers with every intention of using their work as a basis for the forcible imposition of a foreign Catholic monarch upon England" (English Reformation. A.G.Dickens. p.311). In the summer of 1580 a Jesuit mission headed by Edmund Campion and Robert Parsons arrived in England. The Jesuits were controlling the English College in Rome where Dr. William Allen was, and now came to lead the Counter-Reformation. Campion was arrested in June 1581 after moving secretly about the country. At his trial he professed to be purely a missionary for his religion. Yet the Pope's Bull enjoined on him the duty of deposing the reigning sovereign. "So long as heads of Churches claimed this power over heads of States, so long would it be possible for one honest man to call treason, what another called religion" (Tudor England. S.T.Bindoff. p.241). So while Edmund Campion laboured to recover England for the Roman Catholic Faith, he was executed at Tyburn on 1st December 1581 for treason. "He and his fellow workers were labouring to recover England for a Faith, which once enthroned, would have done again, what it had done under Mary, have burnt Dissenters as heretics. Elizabeth burnt only four persons for heresy and none was a Catholic" (Tudor England. S.T.Bindoff. p.241). But she went on to punish those whose actions threatened the State.

The Babington Plot

The great fear of the English Statesmen was that their sovereign, Queen Elizabeth, might fall victim to the assassin's pistol. There was no question that men like Dr. William Allen and his friends were implicated in various plots to destabilise the Monarchy in England. "By 1575 he was already deep in a plot to rescue Mary Queen of Scots by force of arms and turn out the woman whom he had come to regard as a tyrant and a usurper" (The Defeat of the Spanish Armada. Garrett Mattingly. p.67). This man, later to be made a Cardinal by the Pope, worked in conjunction with the Jesuit, Robert Parsons, who had been in England with Edmund Campion. Both men were deeply involved in persuading the

Pope and Philip II of Spain of the urgent need for "foreign intervention" in Britain to overthrow Elizabeth and replace her on the throne by the Catholic, Mary Queen of Scots, who had for 18 years been Elizabeth's prisoner. In 1586 Anthony Babington and some friends conspired to release Mary Queen of Scots and assassinate Elizabeth. This followed a previous conspiracy of a similar nature, the Ridolfi Plot, which had been uncovered in 1571. Mary Queen of Scots, a devout Roman Catholic was first in line for the succession if Elizabeth died, since no children of Henry VIII had any heirs and her claim to the throne came through her grandmother, sister of Henry VIII. The danger for Elizabeth was great. In a secret communication with Philip II in the summer of 1585, Mary had agreed to transfer the succession rights from her son to Philip. Elizabeth's Government had been privy to this letter. Elizabeth had Mary tried for implication in the Babington plot and after much hesitation, signed the Order-in-Council for her execution which was carried out at Fotheringay, where she was beheaded on 8th February 1587. The death sentence was for "incitement to insurrection" and "high treason". In her will Mary declared Philip II of Spain as her heir and not her son James VI of Scotland, who was a Protestant. Her motto was, "My end is my beginning". In her death, she left the Roman Catholic nations of Europe to take up her cause as a Catholic martyr. This caused Philip II of Spain to move to avenge her death and establish his claim to the English throne through his first wife, "Bloody Mary", and through the will of Mary Queen of Scots.

Preparations for the Armada

In 1580, Philip II had taken over Portugal as part of his Empire, together with its fleet. Now with the great wealth of silver which was coming to Spain from America, he prepared to organise "the Great Enterprise". The aim was to conquer Britain and set up a new Roman Catholic Government there. After various plans had been considered it was finally decided to use a fleet of about 130 ships. It was to comprise about 40 warships with about 2,500 guns. In convoy with this fleet were to be 40 large merchant ships and a considerable number of smaller ships. It would be manned by about 8,000 sailors and carry an army of around 22,000 men. With it would go a dozen doctors, 180 priests and churchmen, 19 justices and 50 administrators, who would set up a new Government in England. There were also to be about 150 sons of the nobility together with 700 servants (The Armada. Mary Connatty. p.17). The original plan of the first Commander, Admiral Santa Cruz, (he died in February 1586 and was replaced by the Duke of Medina Sidonia) had been for 500 ships and 60,000 soldiers. This was reduced on the basis of a plan that half the army would be sent over to England from the French coast at Calais under the command of the Duke of Parma. It was planned that this army of Parma, already fighting in the Netherlands, would be withdrawn and shipped by barges out to the Armada and under the protection of the Spanish warships would be taken with the rest of the army to land on the Kent coast near Margate. Thus an invasion force of at least 50,000 troops would be put ashore. Elizabeth was already helping the Dutch fight the Spaniards, having sent a small army under the Earl of Leicester to the Netherlands. If Philip II could capture England, it would make the re-conquest of the Netherlands that much easier. So the extensive organisation of ships, men, stores, and ammunition went ahead to produce the first of the many amphibious operations that the English Channel was to witness as the centuries passed. And as other commanders were to prove, the Channel was a very dangerous zone in which to attempt such a combined operation. The great weakness of the Spanish plan was its duality of purpose. Had Philip first attempted a great naval battle and destroyed the English fleet, then he could have followed it up with a military invasion. Naval supremacy was essential for such an operation to begin. As it was, he combined the naval and military operations into one and hampered his fleet in its naval engagements, at the same time exposing his army to attack. Another great weakness of the Armada was the lack of liaison between its Commander, the Duke of Medina Sidonia, and the Duke of Parma and his army in the Netherlands. There was no deep water port on the coast of Flanders from which a transfer of the troops of the Duke of Parma to the Armada could take place, and the Dutch "Sea Beggars" saw to it that the Spanish barges could not put to sea to join the Spanish Fleet. The Duke of Parma had warned of this danger but neither Philip II nor the Duke of Medina Sidonia had seriously considered the problem. It was a major tactical blunder.

The English Fleet

In the months of preparation before the sailing of the Armada, the English were not idle. The Queen had appointed her cousin, Lord Howard of Effingham, as Lord High Admiral of her Navy, with his

Second-in-Command the great sea captain, Sir Francis Drake, who commanded the 500-ton warship, "Revenge", with Sir John Hawkins, Rear-Admiral in the "Victory". The British Fleet numbered only 34 warships, backed up by 160 hastily armed merchant ships (the little ships) supplied by various ports (Short History of the Royal Navy. A.C.Hampshire. p.15). It was divided into two Squadrons, the Western Fleet based at Plymouth, the Eastern Fleet stationed in The Downs, working in conjunction with a flotilla of ships from the Netherlands. The spirit of patriotism (so lacking in men like Dr. William Allen and Robert Parsons), the sense of purpose and the realisation of danger were the same as that when "the little ships" brought back our army from the Dunkirk beaches in 1940. The danger was equally great in that the whole ideology and culture of this country was at stake from this Spanish Catholic invasion as it was to be from Hitler. Defeat meant inevitably that persecution would return and the fires of Smithfield would burn again. The Spanish Government in doing its propaganda had published a list of the cargo of the Armada, amongst which was included instruments of torture.

Singeing the King of Spain's Beard
    In April 1587, Drake had taken a fleet of 23 ships, 6 from the English Fleet and the rest armed merchant ships, carrying a force of Royal troops, to attack the Armada as it was being prepared in its home ports. His attack on Cadiz Harbour destroyed about 30 ships. Lisbon was blockaded for a month and a final sortie out to the Azores so alarmed the Spaniards that they despatched part of the Armada fleet to protect their shipping in the Atlantic. The whole expedition has come down in history as "the singeing of the King of Spain's beard". It delayed the sailing of the Armada for at least a year and was a supremely successful naval tactic allowing Elizabeth more time to prepare for the invasion.

The Armada Sails
    The Armada eventually sailed out of Lisbon in May 1588. Strong North West winds forced it to take shelter along the coast and to reassemble at Corunna. From here a month later, it again set sail and appeared off The Lizard on 29th July 1588. "A magnificent and awe-inspiring sight it must have been" (Tudor England. S.T.Bindoff. p.273) – this large fleet moving forward in crescent formation – its principal warships line-abreast leading the way, the bulk of the fleet lying to the rear and centre, two

squadrons of warships towards the rear on each flank, the whole spread out over an area of 7 miles. As they came in sight, so the first beacons were lit and from hill to hill across the country to Dover and on to Nottingham, York and Durham, the beacons signalled that the Armada had arrived. The orders of Philip II to Medina Sidonia were clear. He was to make for Flanders and link up with the Duke of Parma. There was no question of any landing being attempted at Plymouth, Southampton or elsewhere along the coast. With a superb discipline, the great fleet kept its tight formation moving along the coast with the English Fleet line ahead, pursuing it, the wind blowing from a Westerly direction and thus enabling the English to win "the weather gauge", and keep to the windward of their enemy, while they attacked them.

The Early Stages of the Conflict

The English understood the Spanish discipline over their fleet; the Spanish realised that the English ships were smaller, yet faster and more nimble than theirs. On shore, the country was ready. An army was mustering under the direction of Leicester at Tilbury, ready to defend the capital. The militia of the Midlands were gathering to London, while those of the South and East were ready to resist any invasion of their shores. Many of the men of Leicester's Force already had fought against Parma's Army in the Netherlands. Restoration work had taken place to various castles and defences along the coast at Plymouth, the Isle of Wight, Southampton, Portsmouth, Deal, Dover and in the Thames Estuary. Basically Elizabeth had the full support of her people. The guns of the English Fleet were long range, and an entirely new type of naval warfare was about to be enacted in the Channel as the English ships, instead of moving up against the enemy ships with broadsides, and using grappling irons to board them and fight on the decks, now moved in line ahead, giving broadsides from a distance, and then withdrawing, thus stopping the Spaniards from coming to grips with the English Fleet. Various skirmishes took place as the Armada moved slowly up the Channel. The first was off the Eddystone, as the English Fleet came out of Plymouth. Further up the coast as the Spanish Fleet moved forward The Rosario was damaged in a collision with one of its own ships and was captured by Drake and towed to Torbay. Later the "San Salvador" blew up and was abandoned and taken to Weymouth. The next battle took place off Portland Bill on 2nd August, and a further one off the Isle of Wight on 4th August, but though the Spanish ships were damaged, none was sunk or put out of action. The Spanish were frustrated at being unable to board any English ship – the English were frustrated at the intense discipline of the Spanish Fleet as it kept its formation moving slowly forward in convoy to Calais. Both sides were expending large amounts of powder and ammunition with little result. One cause for satisfaction for the English was that Plymouth, the Solent and Portsmouth had been passed by and left alone. Gradually the Armada made for the opposite coastline to anchor off Calais on 6th August.

The Great Victory

Now, as the Armada lay at anchor, preparatory to joining up with Parma's Army, the English saw their opportunity. The Western Fleet under Lord Howard had been joined by the Eastern Fleet of 35 ships under Lord Henry Seymour. The Eastern Fleet had been cruising between Dover and Dunkirk, while the Armada came up the Channel, to forestall any early attempt of Parma to move his Army across the Channel. Now the two fleets joined and at midnight on 7th August, Howard sent 8 fireships among the anchored Spanish Fleet. These caused instant panic and for the first time the Armada broke its tight formation and scattered, as these burning ships with their guns firing, drifted towards them on the tide. At dawn on 8th August the English Fleet moved in off Gravelines and "that day was fought one of the decisive battles of history" (Tudor England. S.T.Bindoff. p.275). For 8-9 hours the Spanish ships were pounded. Three of the largest sank. Hundreds of men were killed and injured. Wind and rain ended the battle in the evening and then the danger was that the Armada would founder on the sands off the coast, but by daylight on 9th August the wind had changed, allowing it to make for the open sea. The English had barely lost 100 men, but were desperately short of ammunition, as were the Spaniards. With no port in which to take his fleet and the Channel barred behind him, Medina Sidonia was forced to take his fleet up into the North Sea and face the route round Scotland and Ireland as his only line of retreat to Spain. The wind which had blown off Gravelines now added to the catastrophe of the Armada in the North Sea, as numerous badly damaged ships were overwhelmed by the winds and waves. Others were battered by Atlantic gales and wrecked on the coasts of Scotland and Ireland. The English Western Fleet under Howard followed to the Firth of Forth, while Lord Seymour patrolled the Dover area to watch Parma's movements. Of the major Spanish ships that passed The Lizard on 29th July about 24 never returned. Of the 130 ships of the entire fleet, less than half made it back to Spain and probably only about one-third of the men got home. As with the Battle of Britain, the threat was averted and England breathed a sigh of relief and on the thirtieth anniversary of her Coronation in December 1588, Queen Elizabeth rode in state to St. Paul's Cathedral with her statesmen, bishops and people to return thanks in the language of Psalm 147 v.18, "He causeth His wind to blow", and Psalm 89 v.10, "Thou hast scattered Thine enemies". Whatever was or was not decided by the Battle of Gravelines and the defeat of the Armada, and historians have varying opinions on the subject, one thing was clear: "The defeat of the Armada was decisive – it decided that religious unity was not to be imposed by force on the heirs of Medieval Christendom" (The Defeat of the Spanish Armada. Garrett Mattingly. p.336). There can be absolute certainty that the prayers of many godly Elizabethans, who had already seen exile for their Faith, were signally answered in the great victory, a clear parallel to the answer to the day of National Prayer called by King George VI at the time of Dunkirk, when the seas of the Channel remained calm and 335,000 men came home safely in "the little ships". We have cause to remember the great victory of Gravelines on 8th August 1588 and its consequences for Britain.

Note: The Julian & Gregorian Calendars
In various books readers will come across differences of dating. These are the differences between the Julian Calendar introduced in 46 B.C. and the Gregorian Calendar introduced in Europe in 1582 and in England in 1751. Known as Old Style and New Style there is a variation of 10 days between the two, New Style being 10 days ahead of Old Style. Europeans always dated the Armada by New Style, but the Elizabethans themselves dated it by Old Style. Throughout this account we have used New Style dating. The Spanish dated the Battle of Gravelines as 8th August 1588 (New Style). The Elizabethans dated it 29th July 1588 (Old Style).

Recommended Reading
The Defeat of the Spanish Armada – Garrett Mattingly, 1959.
Tudor England – S.T.Bindoff, 1950.
Europe Divided – J.H.Elliott, 1968.
The English Reformation – A.G. Dickens, 1964.

CHAPTER 2

The Glorious Revolution – 1688

The Succession

1988 marks the 300th anniversary of "The Glorious Revolution". The centuries that have elapsed since then make for a clearer view of the significance of this bloodless Revolution, which changed the succession to the Throne. James II and his baby son James Francis Edward, Prince of Wales (born 10th June 1688) went into exile and a Convention Parliament offered the Throne on condition of "The Declaration of Rights" to Mary, daughter of James II and her husband Prince William of Orange (the Stadtholder of Holland), with her sister Anne as next in the royal line. This upheaval in the succession has only one other parallel in recent history, namely the break in the immediate succession caused by the beheading of Charles I in 1649; but with the accession of Charles II in 1660 the normal line continued. After the 1688 Revolution, the normal line was never restored, even though there was an opportunity for it in 1714 when Queen Anne died without an heir. In 1700, when the Duke of Gloucester – the 11 year-old son and heir of Queen Anne – died, Parliament moved to decide the succession question by the Act of Settlement (1701). The choice rested upon the Protestant Sophia, widow of Ernest Augustus, Elector of Hanover, whose mother Queen Elizabeth of Bohemia was sister of King Charles I. Other claimants included the Roman Catholic James II and his son, and the Roman Catholic Duchess of Savoy, Anna Maria, whose mother Henrietta, Duchess of Orleans was a daughter of Charles I, and sister to Charles II and James II. In fact, Sophia died in 1714 at the same time as Queen Anne and the succession went to her son George, Elector of Hanover, who became King George I.

Constitutional Developments

This explains briefly the significant alterations in the line of succession and raises the question of the reasons and causes for such changes. The initial question is whether there is ever a sufficient reason to remove a Monarch from the throne. The Anglican Church followed a line of non-resistance and considered there was never a sufficient cause to justify the removal of a Monarch. In the 17th Century a body of opinion in the country felt to have a sufficient reason to execute Charles I, "That man of blood," on account of the Civil Wars into which the country had been plunged by him. In 1688 an even larger body of opinion in the country felt it had good reason to call William of Orange from Holland with an army to force James II into exile. Constantly throughout the 17th century there was conflict between the Stuart Kings and their Parliaments. Parliament was developing as a force within the Constitution. Members of the House of Commons felt it to be their right to criticise the actions of the monarchs. This growth and development of the House of Commons had been progressing slowly since the middle of the 16th Century, especially in the reign of Elizabeth I. The Tudor and Stuart Kings, men like Henry VII and James I, had governed as relatively absolute monarchs. Gradually the voice and conscience of the nation was being heard in the House of Commons. Shrewd rulers like Elizabeth I learnt how to guide and lead her Commons. Less shrewd monarchs like Charles I brought about situations of confrontation which led in the 17th Century to Parliament taking up arms against the King and gaining the victory on the battlefield. But when the Constitution had been rocked by this Revolution and no satisfactory alternative Government could be found, in 1660 the Monarchy was restored and Parliament again functioned but never quite as before. In 1660 Parliament was in a stronger position and King Charles II in a weaker one, compared with the situation prior to 1640. Yet still the Stuart Monarchs, Charles II (1660–85) and James II (1685–88), regarded themselves as having a large degree of absolute power in the affairs of State and the conflict continued for 25 years between Parliament and the Monarchy. The basic issues of contention, were who should control taxation and the armed forces; what degree of freedom of speech and freedom of religion should be allowed; who should have the final control, King or Parliament.

The Right to Dissent

The 16th and 17th Centuries saw alternating periods of toleration and persecution as concepts of liberty slowly developed. It was like a tide that ebbed and flowed. Sometimes as in the reign of "Bloody Mary" great waves of persecution swept the land. At other periods, though not entirely eliminated, yet as in the reign of Elizabeth, it had definitely receded to a large degree. The conflict was between the Reformation and the Counter-Reformation, between an absolutist Monarchy and the embryo of Parliamentary democracy. The Puritans of the 16th and 17th

Centuries were a growing, dynamic force in the nation, asserting the right to dissent from the establishment in Church and State. The Thirty Nine Articles of the Church of England stood for "The Protestant Reformed Religion" of the Coronation Oath. "The Westminster Confession of Faith" called for by Parliament in 1643 and approved by them in 1648 represented a clear doctrinal statement of English Puritanism and Scots Presbyterianism, by far the clearest statement of Reformation doctrine. Oliver Cromwell had shown a very large measure of toleration in freedom of speech and religion and liberty of conscience (England in the 17th Century. M. Ashley. p.103), and sincerely desired to restore Parliamentary Government, though he was never able to establish a House of Commons in which he had sufficient confidence to enable him finally to transfer his autocratic powers to it.

Persecution

With the Restoration of the Monarchy in 1660, the seeds of persecution began to appear again. In 1662 the Act of Uniformity drove out about 2,000 clergymen from the National Church in what was known as "The Great Ejection," for refusing to accept a Revised Prayerbook. Puritanism was largely ejected from the Anglican Church on "Black St. Bartholomew's Day 1662", and there then followed bitter persecution by the Anglicans and the Monarchy to stamp out Protestant Nonconformity in the nation. John Bunyan, the 300th Anniversary of whose death is commemorated in 1988 on 31st August, spent 12 years in prison at Bedford for refusing to stop preaching. Various Acts of Parliament, including the Corporation Act 1661, the Conventicle Act 1664 and the Five Mile Act 1665, were used to exclude, hound and harry those who did not conform to the Anglican Church in England and Scotland. There followed a quarter of a century of fines, imprisonments, and persecutions in which not a few gave their lives in martyrdom for their faith and their right to religious freedom. The Clarendon Code, the name by which these Acts and this policy of persecution were known, continued until "The Glorious Revolution" in 1688, with one or two periods of intermission, when the Monarch saw fit to grant a Declaration of Indulgence.

'A Roman Catholic breeze'

By 1670 "a Roman Catholic breeze was blowing through the English Court." (England in the 17th Century. M. Ashley. p.129). Charles II's mother, Henrietta Maria (daughter of Henry IV of France) had been a

Roman Catholic. His brother, James Duke of York, later King James II was received into the Roman Catholic Church in 1669 and ceased to attend the Anglican Communion in 1672. In June 1670 Charles II concluded the Secret Treaty of Dover with France when his sister Henrietta Anne (wife of the Duke of Orleans, brother of Louis XIV of France) came over on a private visit. By it he agreed to become a Roman Catholic and declare it publicly and Louis XIV promised him money and soldiers "to enforce the re-conversion of England to the Faith." "This Treaty was signed by four of his ministers, Arundel, Bellasys, Arlington and Clifford of whom the first two were Roman Catholics in life and the other two at death." (England in the 17th Century. M. Ashley. p.130). Whether Charles II was serious in his intention to convert England to the Catholic Faith is not fully clear, but whatever view is taken, the Treaty was "one of the most discreditable instruments in the history of English Diplomacy." (England in the 17th Century. M. Ashley. p.130). In 1672 Charles II issued a Declaration of Indulgence, suspending the Penal Laws against Nonconformists and Roman Catholics. Nonconformists benefited, though the main purpose of the King was to assist Roman Catholics. But Parliament when called early in 1673 demanded the withdrawal of the Declaration of Indulgence and in return for a vote of money the King gave way and restored the Penal Laws against Nonconformity, agreeing also to the Test Act by which every holder of office, military or civil, should be a communicant member of the Church of England and by this Act James, Duke of York, who was Lord High Admiral was forced to resign his office. When Parliament went further and tried to make sure that the Duke of York's children should be brought up in the Protestant Faith, the King in February 1674 prorogued the Parliament. In 1675, and in February and August 1676, Charles proceeded to sign further secret treaties with France. In the last treaty he took more money from France so that he would be able to govern without Parliament.

The Final Years of Charles II

Mysteriously, after these secret treaties with France, in 1677 Charles agreed to the marriage of his brother, James Duke of York's 14 year-old daughter, Mary, to the Protestant William of Orange, one of France's greatest enemies. There then followed the so-called Popish Plot (of 1677) revealed by Titus Oates and Israel Tonge, which purported to reveal that Jesuits were about to murder Charles II. While much of the information given was untrue, the result was a great wave of fear and anti-Catholic feeling, which in view of the existence of the Secret Treaty of Dover of 1670 was not entirely unjustified. In May 1679 Parliament attempted to exclude the Duke of York from the succession and lay it down that if Charles died without issue, he should be succeeded by a Protestant. To avoid this being passed, the King prorogued and dissolved Parliament. The Parliamentary opposition now found a Protestant successor for the Monarchy in the person of the Duke of Monmouth, the illegitimate son of Charles II and Lucy Walter, his mistress, who in June 1678 had been in charge of the Force that put down the rising of the Scottish Covenanters at Bothwell Bridge. As Charles always supported the legitimate right of his brother James to succeed him, he sent the Duke of Monmouth into exile for a while. In 1680 the House of Commons tried to pass the Exclusion Bill again but it was rejected by the House of Lords. The King eventually dissolved this second Exclusionist Parliament and entered into another secret treaty with France (1681) in return for French financial help, and then summoned a new Parliament at Oxford, but this Parliament was as defiant of the Monarch as ever and after one week was dissolved. The King now ruled without Parliament until the end of his reign. In June 1683 a purported plot was revealed to assassinate Charles, known as the Rye House Plot and while some leading noblemen were executed, there was little real evidence to show that there existed a genuine plot. As his reign drew to its close, Charles ruled by himself and had a standing army and had reached "a position of commanding authority never touched by his Stuart predecessors." (England in the 17th Century. M. Ashley. p.151). On his death bed a Roman Catholic priest came to administer extreme unction to Charles II, and he died in the Roman Catholic Faith on 6th February 1685. King James II quietly succeeded him as a Roman Catholic Monarch.

James II succeeds peacefully
At that moment in time, royal absolutism was in the ascendancy, and it seemed that eventually the Anglican Church would be replaced by the Roman Catholic as the established Church. After three attempts by Parliament to exclude him, James II was now King and that peacefully. At his accession, he assured the Privy Council that he would "make it his endeavour to preserve this Government in Church and State as it is now established by law." His future actions gave rise to the suspicion that he had not quite meant what he said. Relying on the doctrine of non-resistance from the Church of England who supported the claims of the

legitimate Monarch, he was crowned by Archbishop Sancroft, but did not take communion in the Coronation Service. Instead he took mass in Whitehall afterwards. Immediately after the Coronation, he called a Parliament. The election returned an overwhelming number of Royalists, partly due to the changing of the Borough Charters by Charles II. A Scottish Parliament which met first, voted for severe penalties against preachers and their conventicles and there followed in Scotland an era of vicious persecution including the savage murder of the Wigtown Martyrs, Margaret Wilson and Margaret MacLachlan on 11th May 1685, tied to a stake in the sea before the incoming tide, for refusing to take the oath abjuring Scotland's Reformation Covenants. The English Parliament met in May 1685 and voted substantial finances, £2 million, making the King independent of his people, dropping their resolution backing the Penal Laws because James made it clear that that subject would anger him; extending the Law of Treason to include anyone moving in either House of Parliament a change in the descent of the Crown; voting a supply of £700,000 to suppress the Monmouth Rebellion and support a standing army. All the means were provided by this Parliament for absolutist government and the furtherance of the aims of the King for a Roman Catholic State. The King's aim was to obtain a repeal of the Habeas Corpus Act and the Test Act, so that his power over his subjects would be absolute and Roman Catholics could be appointed to the important offices in State and Army. The appointment of Roman Catholic Army officers as his reign progressed leaves an impression that if necessary he would have been prepared to use military force to obtain his objects – for when his Parliament disagreed with these appointments, he prorogued it in November 1685.

Two Rebellions (1685)

Meanwhile, within weeks of Coronation of James II, the Earl of Argyle landed in Scotland and on 11th June the Protestant Duke of Monmouth arrived at Lyme Regis in Dorset, both set to overthrow the Monarchy. Very quickly the Scottish rising was stopped and the Earl executed. The Duke of Monmouth collected an Army of 7,000 which included many Nonconformists, among them William Hewling(19) and Benjamin Hewling (22), the grandsons of William Kiffin, a leading London merchant and Particular Baptist Minister. William Hewling landed from Holland with the Duke and 150 followers, and Benjamin joined the Army of Monmouth later. When the Duke was defeated at Sedgemoor on 5th July,

Judge Jefferies was sent to conduct what was known as "the Bloody Assizes" making his way through Somerset and Dorset, hanging 250 "rebels", sending 800 into banishment and slavery across the seas to the West Indies, and having more whipped and imprisoned. One woman (Dame Alice Lisle) was beheaded at Winchester for harbouring a "rebel" and another (Elizabeth Gaunt) was burnt at Tyburn for the same act. The Duke of Monmouth himself was beheaded on Tower Hill. William Hewling was hung at Lyme Regis and buried there on 13th September 1685; his brother Benjamin was hung at Taunton on 30th September 1685 and buried there. In this way James II warned "rebellious" Protestants of what they might expect. The effect of these military successes was to hasten James II in his policy of establishing a Roman Catholic absolutism, as he failed to grasp how close he had been to defeat at Sedgemoor, nor had he understood the extent of the feeling that lay deep in the nation for liberty, freedom of speech and worship, for which many, like the Hewling brothers, had been willing to sacrifice their young lives. The "rebels" who supported Monmouth were loyal Englishmen, fighting for freedom of religion and conscience against what amounted to an absolutist monarch, who had not fully revealed his true colours at that time, who as yet still received the support of the Anglican Church and many of her followers. When the nation as a whole understood the King's purposes, then it would unite and remove him, and the threads of development would once again be taken up, which would lead forward to a Constitutional Monarchy in a freer country.

The Royal Catholicizing Policy

After his conflict with Parliament over the appointment of Catholic officers in the Army, over the presence of a standing army and his efforts to repeal the Test Acts, James II finding this Parliament not to his liking prorogued it on 20th November 1685 and it never met again. "The infatuated King now devoted all his energies to his Catholicizing policy." (England in the 17th Century. M. Ashley. p.169). He proceeded to repeal the Test Acts and the Penal Acts against Nonconformists (Protestant and Catholic) by a Declaration of Indulgence (April 1686) invoking the Royal power to dispense with statute law. This was sanctioned by the Court of the King's Bench (after it had been purged) in the action of Godden v Hales (June 1686) in which 11 out of 12 judges had determined that the King was entitled to exercise the power he claimed to dispense with laws. Using this "dispensing power" he promoted Roman Catholics in the Civil Service, Local Government, at Oxford and Cambridge Universities as well as in the Armed Forces. A Roman Catholic was put in command of the Fleet, the Roman Catholic Earl of Tyrconnel was made Lord Lieutenant of Ireland (January 1687) and another Roman Catholic was made Master of the Ordnance. A Commission of Ecclesiastical Causes was set up in July 1686 in spite of the fact that such Prerogative Courts had been banned by the Long Parliament in 1641. It was used by James to expel the Fellows of Magdalen College, Oxford and turn the College into a Roman Catholic Institution in 1687 and generally to subdue the Anglican Church. In July 1687 he dissolved Parliament and then tried to influence dissenters to support him against the Anglicans. William Penn, the Quaker Leader, was one who worked with him, thinking that Anglicans were a bigger danger to dissenters than Catholics. James's policy was divide and rule. His object was a packed Parliament, which would obey him, and he sent out agents throughout the country to canvass the gentry in the Counties and the middle classes in the Boroughs to find out from the Lords Lieutenant, the Deputy Lords Lieutenant and the Justices of the Peace who would support his plan to repeal the Test Act. His aim was to produce a Parliament that would vote for the establishment of his absolutist Government. One is reminded of Hitler's rise to power through the elections to the Reichstag of March 1933. The policy was identical – dictatorship via corrupted elections.

Causes of The Glorious Revolution (1688)

In September 1687 it became known that Queen Mary, wife of James II, was pregnant and now it was clear that James's Protestant daughters, Mary, wife of William of Orange, and Anne would be out of the immediate line of succession and if there were a male heir, then James knew that his aim of re-Catholicizing England would be a long-term reality. In April 1688 he re-issued The Declaration of Indulgence and told the Bishops to order the clergy to read it to their congregations on two successive Sundays. In May 1688, seven Bishops refused and were sent to the Tower and tried for seditious libel. On 30th June in the midst of great rejoicing, the Law Court acquitted the Bishops and released them. On 10th June a male heir had been born to James II – James Francis Edward, Prince of Wales (later known as the Old Pretender). Now the country saw that the threat of Catholic absolutism was no longer limited to the lifetime of James II. On the day of the acquittal of the Bishops, an all-party invitation was sent to William of Orange in Holland signed for the Whig Party by Admiral Edward Russell, Mr Henry Sidney, the 4th Earl of Devonshire, the 12th Earl of Shrewsbury, for the Tory Party by the Earl of Danby, Lord Lumley and Henry Compton, Bishop of London. Before receiving this call, William had already decided to invade England and was making preparations for a military invasion. He landed at Brixham in Torbay in Devon on 5th November 1688. In the interval between the all-party call and his landing, James II, realising what was about to happen, panicked and called off the election planned for September 1688. In October 1688 he abolished the Ecclesiastical Commission and at the same time restored the old Charter which he had taken away from the City of London and the Charters of other Cities. He also restored the Fellows of Magdalen College, Oxford and generally attempted to appease the country and the Anglican Church. But it was all too late. As William landed, so the country began to rise in his support, though James still had his fleet and an army twice the size of William's army. Having given the Papal Nuncio a public reception in 1687 and placed his Jesuit advisor, Father Petre on the Privy Council, he had alerted the Anglican Church, the Aristocracy and the whole nation to his fullest intentions. "His most trusted advisers saw that he was blowing the lid off the stove." (England in the 17th Century. M. Ashley. p.170). After all, Roman Catholics were a minority in the country, and the Revocation of the Edict of Nantes in France in October 1685 and the terrible persecution that had followed it, including the exile of 50,000 Huguenots in Britain and 60,000 in Holland had given the Protestant majority in this country and in Holland a clear indication of what the Roman Catholic absolutism of Louis XIV was capable. France virtually wiped out her Huguenot Protestant minority. What would happen to Protestants in England, Scotland and Ireland if James had his own way? Nonconformists in England and the Covenanters in Scotland had felt only too well the intolerance of James II and his brother Charles II.

The Glorious Revolution
   As soon as William landed at Brixham on 5th November 1688, a series of risings followed throughout the country. On 15th November Lord Delamere rose in Cheshire; on 21st November the Earl of Devonshire seized Nottingham; on 22nd November the Earl of Danby took York; on 24th November John Churchill (Victor of the Battle of Sedgemoor and future Duke of Marlborough) defected from the Army; on 25th November Princess Anne, daughter of James II, fled from London to join the

Earl of Danby at York. James came as far as Salisbury on 19th November to meet William and then retreated to London on 26th November. On 28th November he issued a Proclamation for a Parliament and a General Pardon. On 9th December he sent the Queen and his baby son to France and tried to escape himself on 10th/11th December, but was recognised at Faversham in Kent and brought back to London. William entered the capital on 18th December while the King was still there. The King appears to have been asked to leave and allowed to make a successful escape on 23rd December. This he did partly of his own accord, partly under a certain amount of pressure. His presence in the capital was a serious embarrassment to William and there was no desire to arrest or try him. He certainly did not abdicate, as Parliament later decreed. In fact, the Convention Parliament deposed and expelled him from the throne and appointed William of Orange and Mary to the "vacant" throne. As a result of this, the right of the Jacobites was established in their claim to the throne for the old Pretender James, Prince of Wales and the young Pretender Charles Edward in the risings of 1715 and 1745, established on the basis that James II did not abdicate officially. By December 1688 James II's position had become untenable and he had already voluntarily attempted to flee the country once (11th December) and had he been successful on that occasion, it would have been true that he had "deserted" the throne, which would have been tantamount to abdication. As it was with the invading army surrounding the capital, and a majority of his people including his Parliament and his two daughters being against him, his only line of escape would have been to relinquish his absolutist powers and bow before Parliament. The last of the Stuart Kings like his father before him, chose the path of self-sacrifice – he refused to bow, maintaining his legitimacy and absolutist power – the Divine Right of Kings.

The Convention Parliament

On 26th December 1688 the Lords and Bishops, numbering about 90 with an assembly of all who had sat in Charles II's Parliaments with the Lord Mayor of London and the Common Council requested the Prince of Orange to take upon himself the administration of the country following the King's second flight three days before, and issued writs for a Convention Parliament. This Parliament met on 22nd January 1689. It then officially requested the Prince of Orange to take over the administration and the revenue, and on 28th January 1689 after a debate, it came to its great vote, "That King James II, having endeavoured to subvert the constitution of this kingdom, by breaking the original contract between King and people, and by the advice of Jesuits and other wicked persons having violated the fundamental laws, and having withdrawn himself out of the kingdom, has abdicated the Government, and that the throne is thereby vacant". They also resolved unanimously on the next day, "That it hath been found by experience inconsistent with the safety and welfare of this Protestant kingdom to be governed by a Popish Prince." After considerable debate on this resolution and an agreement by the Commons to omit the Clause, "The throne is thereby vacant" and after some discussion in the Lords regarding the possibility of a Protestant Regency, and an amendment to change "abdication" to "desertion", the Commons resolution was finally accepted by the Lords using the word "abdicate" in a very general sense, and the final resolution of 13th February 1689 was extended to include the following words, "That William and Mary, Prince and Princess of Orange, be and be declared, King and Queen of England, France and Ireland, and the dominions there unto belonging, to hold the crown and dignity of the said kingdoms and dominions to them, the said Prince and Princess, during their lives, and the life of the survivor of them; and that the sole and full exercise of the regal power be only in, and executed by, the said Prince of Orange, in the names of the said Prince and Princess, during their joint lives; and after their decease the said crown and royal dignity of the said kingdoms and dominions to be to the heirs of the body of the said Princess; for default of such issue, to the Princess Anne of Denmark, and the heirs of her body; and for default of such issue, to the heirs of the body of the said Prince of Orange." (Constitutional History of England. H. Hallam Vol.III p.98).

"The Declaration of Rights"

This declaration was followed on 18th February by a "Declaration of Rights" presented to Prince William of Orange in the presence of both Houses of Parliament. It consisted of three parts. A recital of illegal and arbitrary acts committed by James II and the consequent vote regarding abdication. Secondly a declaration stating that such acts are illegal and thirdly a resolution that the throne was now filled by the Prince and Princess of Orange according to the limitations stated in the Declaration of Illegalities. The statement reads, "The Lords and Commons in this instrument declare: (a) That the pretended power of suspending laws, and the execution of laws, by regal authority without consent of Parliament is illegal. (b) That the pretended power of dispensing with laws by regal authority, as it hath been assumed and exercised of late is illegal. (c) That the commission for creating the late court of Commissioners for Ecclesiastical Causes, and all other Commissions and Courts of the like nature, are illegal and pernicious. (d) That levying of money for or through the use of the crown, by pretence of prerogative without grant of Parliament, for longer time or in any other manner than the same is or shall be granted, is illegal. (e) That it is the right of the subjects to petition the King, and that all commitments or prosecutions for such petitions are illegal. (f) That the raising or keeping a standing Army within the kingdom in time of peace, unless it be with the consent of Parliament, is illegal. (g) That the subjects which are Protestants may have arms for their defence suitable to their condition and as allowed by law. (h) That elections of members of Parliament ought to be free. (i) That the freedom of speech or debates or proceedings in Parliament ought not to be impeached or questioned in any court or place out of Parliament. (j) That excessive bail ought not to be required nor excessive fines imposed, nor cruel and unusual punishments inflicted. (k) That juries ought to be impannelled and returned, and that jurors which pass upon men in trials of high treason ought to be freeholders. (l) That all grants and promises of fines and forfeitures of particular persons, before conviction, are illegal and void. (m) And that for redress of all grievances, and for the amending, and strengthening, and preserving of the laws, Parliaments ought to be held frequently." (Constitutional History of England. H. Hallam. Vol.III. p.102–3).

"The Bill of Rights"

Some months afterwards the Declaration was confirmed by a regular Act of Parliament and became known as "The Bill of Rights" which established at the same time the limitations of the Crown according to the vote of the Lords and Commons and added the important provision, "That all persons who shall hold communion with the Church of Rome, or shall marry a Papist, shall be excluded, and for ever incapable to possess, inherit, or enjoy, the Crown and Government of this realm; and in all such cases, the people of these realms shall be absolved from their allegiance, and the Crown shall descend to the next heir." (H. Hallam. Vol.III. p.103). In "The Bill of Rights" a clause was added allowing a "Dispensing Power" to the Monarch providing a Bill was passed in the then present session of Parliament concurring with the Monarch's action. "The Bill of Rights" condemned James II's use of the "Dispensing Power" under the words, "As it hath been assumed or exercised of late", that is, abused.

Hallam's assessment of the Revolution

Henry Hallam, in his "Constitutional History of England" (Volume III Chapter 15 p. 101) says, "The Revolution is not to be considered as a mere effort of the nation on a pressing emergency to rescue itself from the violence of a particular Monarch, much less as grounded upon the danger of the Anglican Church, its emoluments, and dignities, from the bigotry of a hostile religion. It was rather the triumph of those principles which, in the language of the present day, are denominated liberal or constitutional, over those of absolute Monarchy, or of Monarchy not effectually controlled by stated boundaries. It was the termination of a contest between the regal power and that of Parliament which could not have been brought to so favourable an issue by any other means". It was the culmination of a conflict between King and Parliament in the reigns of the Stuart Kings, Charles I, Charles II and James II. Central to that controversy was the conflict between the Reformation and the Counter-Reformation – central to that controversy was freedom of speech and religion. "The Bill of Rights" was immediately followed by a Toleration Act, which freed Dissenters from penalties for failing to go to Church and abolished many of the punishments of the Clarendon Code, though Nonconformists still were kept out of public office, both civil and military, and the Acts against Roman Catholics remained in force. "By the revolution, and by the Act of Settlement, the rights of the actual Monarch of the reigning family, were made to emanate from Parliament, and the people. In technical language, in the grave and respectful theory of our constitution, the Crown is still the fountain from which law and justice spring forth. Its prerogatives are in the main the same as under the Tudors and the Stuarts; but the right of the House of Hanover, to exercise them can only be deduced from the convention of 1688". (H. Hallam. Vol. III p.91). "Such was the termination of that contest which the House of Stuart had obstinately maintained against the liberties and of late against the religion of England or rather that far more ancient controversy between the Crown and the people, which had never been wholly at rest since the reign of John". (H. Hallam. Vol. III. p.99). This controversy went back to Magna Carta.

The Act of Settlement (1701)

The culmination of the Glorious Revolution came with the Act of Settlement of 1701. Having laid down the succession in "The Bill of Rights" 1689, Parliament went on to clarify it more fully before the death of William and Mary and before the death of Queen Anne who through the death of her son, the 11 year-old Duke of Gloucester, was without an heir. Eight articles were inserted in the Act of Settlement to take effect only from the commencement of the new limitation of the House of Hanover. The articles of this Act are as follows: "(1) That whosoever shall hereafter come to the possession of this Crown shall join in communion with the Church of England as by law established. (2) That in case the Crown and imperial dignity of this realm shall hereafter come to any person, not being a native of this kingdom of England, this nation be not obliged to engage in any war for the defence of any dominions or territories which do not belong to the Crown of England without the consent of Parliament. (3) That no person who shall hereafter come to the possession of this Crown, shall go out of the dominions of England, Scotland or Ireland without consent of Parliament. (4) That from and after the time that the further limitation by this Act shall take effect, all matters and things relating to the well-governing of this kingdom, which are properly cognizable in the Privy Council by the laws and customs of this realm, shall be transacted there, and all resolutions taken there upon shall be signed by such of the Privy Council as shall advise and consent to the same. (5) That, after the said limitation shall take effect as aforesaid, no person born out of the kingdoms of England, Scotland or Ireland, or the dominions there unto belonging (although he be naturalised or made a denizen – except such as are born of English parents), shall be capable to be a member of the Privy Council, or a member of either House of Parliament, or to enjoy any office or place of trust, either civil or military, or to have any grants of lands, tenements, or hereditaments from the Crown to himself or to any other or others in trust for him. (6) That no person who has an office or place of profit under the King or receives a pension from the Crown shall be capable of serving as a member of the House of Commons. (7) That after the said limitation shall take effect as aforesaid, judges' commissions be made *quamdiu se bene gesserint* (during good behaviour), and their salaries ascertained and established; but, upon the address of both Houses of Parliament it may be lawful to remove them. (8) That no pardon under the great Seal of England be pleadable to an impeachment by the Commons in Parliament." (H.

Hallam. Vol.III. p.180–181). Article 1 in fact, established the accession of the House of Hanover and finally ruled out any possibility of a return to the Stuarts or any other Roman Catholic Monarch. Article 4 attempted to limit secrecy in Government, which Charles II had used so much, and made certain that all Government business was done openly in the Privy Council and signed openly by all the members present. Article 7 appointed judges for life, that is as long as they were competent to administer justice, established the independence of the judiciary and made them removable only by Parliament.

Results of the Glorious Revolution

James II and his Jacobite followers made various efforts to recover his throne. The first was when he landed in Ireland in March 1690 with French troops. This attack was marked by the heroic success of Londonderry which withstood a siege from April to August 1690, and by James's defeat at the Battle of the River Boyne on 11th July 1690, after which he returned to France and remained there on a pension from Louis XIV until his death on 6th September 1701. This invasion was followed by Jacobite risings in 1715 and 1745. But all failed to restore Stuart absolutism. The Glorious Revolution takes its name from this bloodless break in the line of succession, and with it England entered a new era – the era of Parliamentary Government. If political freedom was not obtained by all, neither was religious freedom. Nonconformity obtained religious freedom but not political. Roman Catholics obtained neither, though some relaxation was allowed later. "The Act of Settlement was the seal of our Constitutional Laws, the complement of the revolution itself and the Bill of Rights, the last great statute which restrains the power of the Crown, and manifests, in any conspicuous degree, a jealousy of Parliament in behalf of its own and the subject's privileges". (H. Hallam. Vol. III p.196). This was the basis of the Protestant Constitution of this country enshrined in the Coronation Oath which the Monarch swears prior to the enthronement in Westminster Abbey. The Archbishop in administering the Coronation Oath, first asks the Monarch, "Is your Majesty willing to take the Oath?" And the Monarch answering, "I am willing", the Archbishop then asks the King three questions, demanding of him first, if he will solemnly promise and swear to govern his people according to the laws and customs of the Constitution; secondly, if he will do his best to cause law and justice, in mercy, to be executed in all his judgements; thirdly, if he will to the utmost of his power maintain the

Laws of God, the true profession of the Gospel and the Protestant Reformed Religion established by law, and also maintain and preserve the Church of England and the rights and privileges of the bishops and clergy and the Churches committed to their charge. To each of these questions, the Monarch gives his solemn assent, and then rising out of his chair he goes to the Altar, attended by two Bishops and the Lord Great Chamberlain, the Sword of State being carried before him. There he makes his Oath in the sight of all the people laying his right hand upon the Holy Gospel in the Great Bible and says, "The things which I have here before promised, I will perform, and keep. So help me God." Then the King kisses the Book and signs the Oath. In this solemn manner the Monarch takes the Coronation Oath to uphold "the Protestant Reformed Religion established by law." Also on the accession each Monarch takes the Accession Oath before the Privy Council as follows, "I do solemnly and sincerely in the presence of God, profess, testify, and declare that I am a faithful Protestant, and that I will according to the true intent of the enactments which secure the Protestant succession to the Throne of my Realm, uphold and maintain the said enactments to the best of my powers according to the law." And then the Monarch takes the Oath relating to the security of the Church of Scotland.

In this way "the true intent of the enactments which secure the Protestant succession" has been maintained since "The Glorious Revolution" of 1688 and the Act of Settlement of 1701. "The Settlement of 1689 has stood the test of time." (A History of England. G.M. Trevelyan. p.472). Only now 300 years later, with the movement in the Anglican Communion towards re-union with the Roman Catholic Church, is this Settlement in serious danger.

Recommended Reading
The Constitutional History of England – Henry Hallam 1867
England in the 17th Century – Maurice Ashley 1952
The Monmouth Rebels – W.M. Wigfield 1985
The Monmouth Rebellion – R. Dunning 1984
The Axminster Ecclesiastica – Edit K. Howard 1976

CHAPTER 3

Anglican-Roman Catholic Reunion – 1988

Introduction

The campaign of the Counter-Reformation, to recover Britain for the Roman Catholic Faith, is now about to enter another phase. Protestantism is in a "Dunkirk" situation – all loyal Protestants must be looking to Gideon's God. In the 16th Century, He appeared and the words of Queen Elizabeth on the monument on Plymouth Hoe and on the medal struck to commemorate the defeat of the Armada – "He blew with His wind and they were scattered," – have a contemporary echo. Having failed to conquer the country by force in 1588, having failed to capture the Throne in 1688, this third attempt has been designed to alter the Protestant Constitution by changing the doctrine of the Anglican Church. A Roman Catholic missionary enterprise within the country has been in progress for over 150 years. This has been carefully planned and worked out with great skill and patience. Moves have been made gradually with caution and care to diminish the Protestant Reformed character of the Church of England and introduce into her midst practices and doctrines which tend to Roman Catholicism.

The Oxford Movement

Beginning in Oxford in the 1830's with the formation of the Oxford Movement by such men as John Henry Newman, John Keble, Edward Bouverie Pusey, there has developed throughout the Anglican Communion what has been termed the Anglo-Catholic Movement. Over the last 100 years, Anglican Churches have introduced Roman Catholic ritual and practices such as candles, incense, the reserved sacrament, confessionals, vestments, crucifixes, prayers for the dead, etc., and in the wake of these practices has come Roman Catholic doctrines.

The Royal Family

A cordiality has been developed between the Papacy and the Royal Family. This commenced in the reign of Queen Victoria when she sent a deputation to Rome at the time of the Jubilee of Pope Pius IX in 1877. At the time of her own Jubilee in 1887, gifts were exchanged between Her

Majesty and Pope Leo XIII and envoys carried greetings. Further contacts took place in 1897 at the time of the Queen's Diamond Jubilee. King Edward VII visited Pope Leo XIII in his reign. In 1914, a British Envoy was assigned to the Vatican and in 1923 King George V and Queen Mary paid a visit to the Vatican and were received by Pope Pius XI. In 1924 a similar visit was made by the Prince of Wales. In 1938 an Apostolic Delegation was established in London. Similar visits have been made by succeeding Monarchs and members of the Royal Family until Archbishop Ramsey visited the Vatican in 1966 when it was agreed to set up the Commission, known as ARCIC I – The Anglican Roman Catholic International Commission – to look into ways of overcoming differences between the two Communions and promoting reunion. As gradually over the years Statesmen, Archbishops and Monarchs have visited Rome, it has become standard practice to meet the Pope. A completely new tone of friendly relationships has been established between the Queen as Head of the Anglican Church and the Archbishop of Canterbury, Dr. Runcie towards the Roman Catholic Church. This resulted in the visit of the Pope to this country and his meeting with the Queen at Buckingham Palace in 1982 and his meeting at Canterbury with the Prince of Wales and Dr. Runcie. Simultaneously an Apostolic Nuncio was appointed to this country.

Differences of Doctrine

Other aspects in this development have included important efforts to blend the Thirty Nine Articles of the Church of England with the teaching of the Roman Catholic Church. In 1835 Edward Pusey, a member of the Oxford Movement, published Tract XC, in which he attempted to show that the doctrines of the Thirty Nine Articles could be shown to conflate with Roman Catholic teaching and make it possible for a clergyman to subscribe to them and yet accept much Roman Catholic teaching. In 1927 a Revision was made in the Prayer Book – drawn up and accepted by Convocation and the Church Assembly, with the support of a large majority of Bishops and the House of Lords, yet finally rejected by the House of Commons by 238 votes to 205. The tendency of this Revised Prayer Book was to open the way towards Roman Catholic teaching in the Church of England. In more recent years there has been introduced the Alternative Service Book (1980), which derives its legal status from the Worship and Doctrine Measure of 1974 and in certain places manifests a similar tendency to the Prayer Book of 1927.

Anglican Religious Orders
Another area of influence in the Church of England has been through the formation of Anglo-Catholic Religious Orders and Communities of both men and women. The first Woman's Sisterhood was established in Regents Park, London in 1845 and by 1920 there were at least 40 Women's Communities belonging to the Church of England. Towards the end of the 19th Century, various Male Orders were formed. One of the well-known ones was the Community of the Resurrection formed in 1892 and now centred at Mirfield in Yorkshire since 1898, where the College of the Resurrection was founded in 1902 for training candidates for Ordination. This is now one of the principal training colleges for Anglo-Catholics.

The Spread of Roman Catholicism in Britain
Parallel with the developments around the Throne and in the Church of England, has been a substantial development in the Roman Catholic Church in this country. In 1850 the Roman Catholic Hierarchy of Bishops was established once again in England. The country was divided into Roman Catholic Dioceses and Archbishops and Bishops appointed over them with the Archbishop of Westminster over the whole organisation. Nicholas Wiseman was created Cardinal and sent to England as the new Archbishop of Westminster. Since that time in the intervening century, the Roman Catholic Church has grown in Britain – numbering about 800,000 adherents in 1850, it now numbers about 5,100,000 adherents (2,315,000 regular communicants). In 1867 a site was purchased in London and later Westminster Cathedral was built there. This is the central church in Britain of the Roman Catholic Church. In 1911 Pope Pius X divided England into three Provinces, namely Westminster, Birmingham and Liverpool, each having its own Archbishop, and a fourth Province was made at Cardiff in 1916 with its own Archbishop. In these four Sees there has been about 15 Dioceses. As well as this there has been extensive growth in Roman Catholic Religious Orders and Communities. By 1950 there were in this country 70 Orders of men and 140 Orders of women and under the Government regulations for the new Community Charge, it has been agreed to exempt about 5,000 monks and nuns on the grounds that they have no income. Famous names of their Houses which often are also well-known schools, include Downside, Stoneyhurst, Ampleforth and Buckfast Abbey. One area in which the Roman Catholic Church has made great strides has been in Education with Roman

Catholic Halls at Universities and Teacher Training Colleges spread around the country linked to Universities, sending teachers into the large number of Roman Catholic schools, which in 1960 numbered about 2,500; many of which are private, but a large number also state-aided.

The Ecumenical Movement

These facts and figures demonstrate in some small degree the development of the Counter-Reformation in its set task of recovering the lost province of Northern Europe for the fold of the "one Universal Church". A further feature of this development has been the Ecumenical Movement which has swept the Christian Churches together, culminating in "the historic Church Unity Conference" at Swanwick, Derbyshire, 31st August – 4th September 1987, when 350 of Britain's top Church leaders welcomed a statement by Cardinal Hume, that the Roman Catholics were now ready to give full commitment to Ecumenism. The Conference issued "The Swanwick Declaration" which was read in all Churches during October 1987 and published as a report entitled "Not Strangers but Pilgrims". Centring around the World Council of Churches more recent manifestations are visible at a local level in such concords as "the Wirral Covenant" in which the Bishop of Chester, who has been noted for his Evangelical sympathies, has allied on Merseyside with all denominations, including Roman Catholics. The attitude of the Charismatic (House Church) Movement towards Roman Catholicism opens up some very serious questions. In the U.S.A. it has been a common sight to find Charismatics and Roman Catholics on the same platform. The Pope has received Charismatic leaders from the U.S.A. in private audience and gives the whole movement of tongues and faith healing his blessing. Charismatics feel that if Roman Catholics have the gifts of healing and tongues, then irrespective of their beliefs in the Mass and the Veneration of the Virgin Mary, there is a basis for Christian concord and union. The Ecumenical Movement is based on a declining Christian Church which is seeking to unite on a basis of a minimum amount of doctrine, distinguishing what is regarded as essential from what is non-essential, and while the Roman Catholic Church has kept outside of a full commitment to the World Council of Churches, yet in the Second Vatican Council in 1962, large numbers of leaders of all denominations were present as observers, and since that time the common parlance has been that, "Rome *is* changing". While Anglican Evangelicals, like the Bishop of Chester can give credence to this, then we must seriously ask ourselves, "What is an Evangelical?"

Anglican Roman Catholic International Commission (ARCIC) Proposals
July 1988 sees the discussion by the Lambeth Conference of the Bishops of the Anglican Communion of the ARCIC II document on Justification by Faith, known as, "Salvation and the Church." This is an attempt to conflate the Reformation doctrine of Justification with that expressed by the Roman Catholics at the Council of Trent which met between 1545-1563. This is one of the final stages before reunion can be achieved between the Anglican Communion and the See of Rome. The steps in this process have been going forward since Archbishop Ramsey's visit to Rome in 1966.

ARCIC I
This process began with the meeting of ARCIC I in 1970. After numerous discussions it produced three agreed statements – 1971, "The Eucharist or Lord's Supper" – 1973, "The Ministry" – 1975 and 1981, "Authority in the Church." Put together these three agreed statements constituted the Final Report of ARCIC I published in 1982 just prior to the visit of the Pope to Britain, timed to anticipate the Papal visit to Canterbury. On that visit Dr. Runcie and the Pope agreed to set up a second Commission, to be known as ARCIC II, which would contain a larger number of Evangelical Anglicans than ARCIC I and examine such pertinent causes of division as Justification by Faith and women priests. ARCIC I has been fully debated in the General Synod of the Church of England and at noon on 14th February 1985, the Church of England through its representative body "agreed its willingness to take into its system the office of Universal Primate of Rome" – an historic decision indeed. The report of this decision was accepted in every diocese of the Church of England in this country and was finally agreed again by a significant majority in the General Synod in November 1986. The Synod divides into three Houses – Bishops, Clergy and Laity. It is noteworthy that while the Bishops and the Clergy passed it with substantial majorities, the House of Laity showed a significant resistance to all three agreed statements and the statement on "Authority" came very near to defeat. The chairman of the House of Laity, Professor MacLean, said he was shocked by the strength of the opposition.

The Final Report – 1982

In respect of the agreed statements on the Eucharist (Lord's Supper) and the Ministry, these are said to be "consonant in substance with the Faith of the Church of England – i.e. the Thirty Nine Articles of Religion." In respect to "Authority" it was said, "that the statement provides sufficient convergence to explore further the structure of authority and exercise of Collegiality and Primacy of the Pope, and offers sufficient basis for taking the next concrete steps towards reconciliation of our Churches." In this way a firm commitment was made toward reunion. In the first place it is fair to enquire what exactly the Church of England has accepted in the Final ARCIC Report to which she has already committed herself.

The Lord's Supper (ARCIC I)

Respecting the Lord's Supper ARCIC I makes such statements as, "the Eucharistic Memorial is no mere calling to mind as the New Testament says, of a past event or its significance, but rather it is the making effective in the present of an event in the past." It goes on to say of the Lord's Supper, "we are caught up into and our sacrifice is joined to that of Christ." And again, "the Church enters into the movement of Christ's self-offering." This ambiguous language opens the door to something more than the Zwinglian view of the Lord's Supper as a service of remembrance, and certainly something more than Cranmer intended in his Prayer Book of 1552. Queen Elizabeth I in her Prayer Book of 1562 managed to combine the language of the 1549 Prayer Book (the body of our Lord Jesus Christ which was given for thee) and that of the 1552 Prayer Book (take and eat this in remembrance that Christ died for thee); one of which was semi-Catholic and the other thoroughly Reformed. This is the avenue by which many in the Church of England find themselves able to agree with this type of declaration and agreed statement regarding the Lord's Supper conflating the Book of Common Prayer Communion Service with the Roman Catholic Mass and its doctrine of Transubstantiation.

The Ministry

Regarding the Ministry ARCIC I says, "Despite the fact that New Testament ministers are never called priests, Christians came to see the priestly role of Christ reflected in these ministers and used priestly terms in describing them. Because the Eucharist is the memorial of the sacrifice of Christ, the action of the presiding minister in reciting again the words of Christ at the Last Supper and distributing to the Assembly the holy gifts is seen to stand in a sacramental relation to what Christ Himself did in offering His own sacrifice." Again ARCIC I in ambiguous language opens the door wide for Christian ministers to be seen as priests performing a sacrifice, rather than as the New Testament always describes them as elders (Presbyters), preaching the Gospel. Article 19 of the Thirty Nine Articles faithfully describes the New Testament view, "The visible Church of God is a congregation of faithful men, in which the pure word of God is *preached* and the sacraments be duly ministered according to Christ's ordinance...."

Authority

Finally as regards authority in the Church ARCIC I says, "In a reunited Church there should be a Head and that Head should be the Bishop of Rome." To the Church and the Pope is attributed the quality of "indefectability." The Shorter Oxford Dictionary defines "indefectability" as, "not liable to decay or defect – faultless," and at once it is seen that the concept here is identical to the Roman Catholic teaching on Papal Infallibility, decreed by the Vatican Council in 1870. By this the Pope and the Church are set in a superior position to the Scriptures. Article 6 of the Thirty Nine Articles shows where the Church of England stands; it reads, "Holy Scripture containeth all things necessary to salvation, so that whatsoever is not read therein nor may be proved thereby is not required of any man, that it should be believed as an article of Faith or be thought requisite or necessary for salvation. In the name of the Holy Scripture we do understand those Canonical Books of the Old and New Testament, of whose authority there never was any doubt in the Church." Article 21 says, "General Councils may not be gathered together without the commandment and will of Princes. And when they be gathered together (for as much as they be an assembly of men, whereof all be not governed with the Spirit and Word of God), they may err, and sometimes have erred, even in things pertaining to God. Wherefore things ordained by them as necessary to salvation have neither strength nor authority, unless it be declared that they be taken out of Holy Scripture." This Article 21 effectively removes the necessity of believing such Roman Catholic dogma as Papal Infallibility, and the Assumption and the Immaculate Conception of the Virgin Mary. Article 37 says, "The Queen's Majesty hath the Chief power in the realm of England and her other dominions –

the Bishop of Rome hath no jurisdiction in this realm of England." All this makes sufficiently clear the position of Holy Scripture as the sole foundation of authority for doctrine and practice in the Church of England and the Queen as Head of the Church.

Possible Consequences of ARCIC I

Any change in the doctrine and position of the Church of England will of necessity require alterations to the Act of Settlement (1701) and changes will have to be made in the Accession Oath and the Coronation Oath which can only be effected by Act of Parliament. The Protestant Constitution will be forfeited and the National Church will be of an Ecumenical character under the Primacy of the Pope. It will be very interesting to see if our democratic society will accept a situation in which the Monarch comes under the influence of the Papacy, for it is certain that pressure will be brought to bear on Parliament to rescind many laws which are contrary to Catholic teaching. It appears that while most leaders of the principal Nonconformist Churches (the Church of Scotland, the United Reformed Church, the Baptist and Methodist Churches) and the Anglican Church are ready for this full commitment with Rome for the Ecumenical set-up of "The Swanwick Declaration", there are groups in these denominations who are prepared to withdraw and to stand alone. A whole new divide in Christian Churches in Britain is within sight – once again centring around the Reformation and Counter-Reformation – Protestantism and Catholicism. The decision as to whether the Anglican and Roman Catholic Churches reunite rests finally in the hands of the Monarch and Parliament. May Her Majesty be given wisdom to stand firm and Parliament grasp the immense significance culturally, educationally, politically, and constitutionally for our Protestant Constitution, enshrining the freedoms and the democracy we value and have fought for over the generations, and which we have shared with the Commonwealth. If we cannot have our Protestant Reformed Constitution as established by law, would not the nation rather choose in that situation to follow the example of the United States and have no national Church as established by law?

ARCIC II

The next moves in the reconciliation between the Anglican and Roman Catholic Churches are taking place in 1988. With the Final Report accepted and fully discussed there will now follow consideration of the

ARCIC II document published in 1987 on Justification by Faith entitled, "Salvation and the Church." This comes before the Lambeth Conference in July 1988, and then follows the next Plenary Session of ARCIC II in Ireland in September. If the statement, "Salvation and the Church", is agreed by the Lambeth Conference and accepted by the Synod of the Church of England, then the only outstanding areas that need agreement are such matters as women priests, Indulgences, Mariolatry and the various dogmas such as Infallibility, the Immaculate Conception and Assumption of the Virgin Mary, which have no basis in the Canonical Scriptures (i.e. all Scripture excluding the books of the Apocrypha, which are not divinely inspired).

The Reformed Doctrine of Justification

The doctrine of Justification by Faith was the focal point of the Reformation. The Thirty Nine Articles of the Church of England express it in Article 11 in these words, "We are accounted righteous before God, only for the merit of our Lord and Saviour Jesus Christ by Faith, and not for our own works or deservings; wherefore, that we are justified by Faith only is a most wholesome doctrine, and very full of comfort, as more largely expressed in the Homily of Justification." This Homily by Thomas Cranmer (Archbishop of Canterbury and author of the 1552 Book of Common Prayer) defines the doctrine in this way, "Justification is not the office of man but of God, for man cannot make himself righteous by his own work, neither in part nor in the whole, for that were the greatest arrogance and presumption of man, that Anti-Christ could set up against God, to affirm that a man might by his own works, take away and purge his own sins and so justify himself. But justification is the office of God only, and is not a thing which we render unto Him, but which we receive of Him: not which we give to Him, but which we take of Him, by His free mercy, and by the only merit of His most dearly beloved Son, our only Redeemer, Saviour, and Justifier, Jesus Christ: so that the true understanding of this doctrine, we be justified freely by Faith without works, or that we be justified by Faith in Christ only, is not, that this our own act to believe in Christ, or this our Faith in Christ, which is within us, doth justify us, and deserve our justification unto us (for that were to count ourselves to be justified by some act or virtue that is within ourselves) but the true understanding and meaning thereof is, that although we hear God's Word and believe it, although we have faith, hope, charity, repentance, dread, and fear of God within us, and do never so many works there unto: yet we must renounce the merit of all our said virtues, of faith, hope, charity, and all other virtues and good deeds, which we either have done, shall do, or can do, as things that be far too weak and insufficient, and imperfect to deserve remission of our sins, and our justification, and therefore we must trust only in God's mercy, and that sacrifice which our High Priest and Saviour Christ Jesus the Son of God once offered for us upon the Cross, to obtain thereby God's grace and remission......" Article 12 speaks of the place of good works in relation to Justification and says, "Albeit that good works, which are the fruits of Faith and follow after Justification, cannot put away our sins and endure the severity of God's Judgement; yet are they pleasing and acceptable to God in Christ, and do spring out necessarily of a true and lively Faith; insomuch that by them a lively Faith may be as evidently known as a tree discerned by the fruit."

The Westminster Confession of Faith

The Westminster Confession of Faith, commissioned by Parliament in 1643 and ratified in 1647 expresses the doctrine concisely in these words:–
1. Those whom God effectually calleth, He also freely justifieth: not by infusing righteousness into them, but by pardoning their sins, and by accounting and accepting their persons as righteous; not for anything wrought in them, or done by them, but for Christ's sake alone; nor by imputing Faith itself, the act of believing, or any other Evangelical obedience to them, as their righteousness; but by imputing the obedience and satisfaction of Christ unto them, they receiving and resting on Him and His righteousness by Faith; which Faith they have not of themselves, it is the gift of God.
2. Faith, thus receiving and resting on Christ and His righteousness, is the alone instrument of justification: yet it is not alone in the person justified, but is ever accompanied with all other saving graces, and is no dead Faith, but worketh by love.
3. Christ, by His obedience and death, did fully discharge the debt of all those that are thus justified, and did make a proper, real, and full satisfaction to His Father's justice in their behalf. Yet, in as much as He was given by the Father for them; and His obedience and satisfaction accepted in their stead; and both, freely, not for anything in them; their justification is only of free grace; that both the exact justice, and rich grace of God might be glorified in the justification of sinners.

4. God did, from all eternity, decree to justify all the elect, and Christ did, in the fullness of time, die for their sins, and rise again for their justification: nevertheless, they are not justified, until the Holy Spirit doth, in due time, actually apply Christ unto them.
5. God doth continue to forgive the sins of those that are justified; and although they can never fall from the state of justification, yet they may, by their sins, fall under God's fatherly displeasure, and not have the light of His countenance restored unto them, until they humble themselves, confess their sins, beg pardon, and renew their Faith and repentance.
6. The justification of believers under the Old Testament was, in all these respects, one and the same with the justification of believers under the New Testament.

This statement on Justification of the Westminster Confession is followed exactly word for word in the Savoy Declaration of 1658 of the Congregationalists and Independents, and again in the Baptist Confession of Faith, "Things Most Surely Believed Among Us," of 1689. Thus the Anglican, Presbyterian Churches of England and the Church of Scotland, the Congregationalists and Baptists have all followed in the past in the same steps as Martin Luther when he clearly expounded the doctrine of Justification in his Commentary on Paul's "Epistle to the Galatians."

ARCIC II on Justification – "Salvation and the Church."

The clarity of these Protestant doctrinal statements stands in stark contrast to the ARCIC II agreed statement, "Salvation and the Church." The theory put forward by the members of the Commission, Roman Catholic and Anglican, is that the Reformers and the Catholic theologians of the Council of Trent (1545–1563) misunderstood each other, extremists on each side produced caricatures of each others beliefs. Now, if the Report is to be believed, modern Biblical scholarship, historical and theological studies, new insights from the mission field, and the growth of understanding from the Ecumenical side, with much good will on both sides, have brought each side to a position where no conflict now exists over the doctrine of Justification. This explanation makes a mockery of the Spirit's work in illuminating the hearts of the Reformers. The only way to establish the truth regarding this doctrine is to examine it in the light of the Scriptures. The agreed statement in section 14 has some revealing remarks about this, when dealing with the meaning of the word

Justification. It admits that the Reformers in their interpretation followed the "predominant usage" of the New Testament Greek, while the theologians of the Council of Trent followed the usage of the patristic and medieval Latin writers. It is at this point that the major doctrinal differences have arisen. The Latin "justificare" as found in the Roman Catholic Latin Vulgate Bible signifies "to make righteous." The New Testament Greek verb "dikaioun" means "to pronounce righteous." The Seventeenth Century Protestant theologian, John Owen, (Dean of Christ Church and Vice-Chancellor of the University of Oxford), says categorically, "This (Greek) word is not used in any good (Greek) author whatever to signify the making of a man righteous," but is used to mean "to acquit or pronounce righteous." (The Works of John Owen. Vol.11. Ch.4 p.159. 'Justification by Faith'). The agreed statement (Section 14), allows for both interpretations, instead of clearly stating that the Reformers were right and the Vulgate Latin was a misinterpretation and a mistranslation of the Greek.

John Owen and Richard Hooker on Justification

John Owen in his work on Justification says, "The true and genuine signification of Justification is to be determined from the words of the original languages." (Owen's Works. Vol.XI. Ch.4. p.155). As regards the Hebrew of the Old Testament and the Greek of the Septuagint translation of the Hebrew, he says that, "In no place is the word 'to justify' used in any other sense than to absolve, acquit, esteem, declare, pronounce righteous or to impute righteousness, which is the forensic sense of the word; that is its constant use and signification nor does it ever once signify 'to make inherently righteous'" (Works. Vol.XI. p.156). Roman Catholics maintain that at baptism, grace is infused into the soul, pardoning original sin, which is the commencement of the work of Justification, which is continued in the soul through the sacraments of the Church, Mass, etc., and good works. John Owen says, regarding the translation of 'justificare', "Whatever an infusion of grace may be, or however it may be called Justification, it is not, it cannot be; the word nowhere signifies any such thing." (Works. Vol.XI. p.156). Richard Hooker, the Anglican theologian, quoted in "Salvation and the Church" Section 15, Footnote 2, (author of "The Laws of Ecclesiastical Polity") says in his "Discourse on Justification", (Works of Richard Hooker Edit. W.S. Dobson 1825. Vol.II. p.501–502) regarding justifying righteousness, "This Grace they (Roman Catholics) will have to be applied by infusion; to the end, that as the body is warm by the heat which is in the body, so the soul might be righteous by inherent Grace; which Grace they make capable of increase; as the body may be more and more warm so the soul more and more justified, according as Grace should be augmented; the augmentation whereof is merited by good works, as good works are made meritorious by it. Wherefore the first receipt of Grace in their divinity is the first Justification; the increase thereof, the second Justification. As Grace may be increased by the merit of good works; so it may be diminished by the demerit of sins venial; it may be lost by mortal sin. ..... To such as diminish it by venial sins, it is applied by Holy Water, Ave Marias, Crossings, Papal Salutations, and such like, which serve for reparations of Grace decayed. To such as have lost it through mortal sin, it is applied by the Sacrament of Penance; which Sacrament hath force to confer grace anew, yet in such sort, that being so conferred, it hath not altogether so much power as at the first. For it only cleanses out of the stain or guilt of sin committed, and changeth the punishment eternal into a temporal satisfactory punishment here, if time do serve: if not, hereafter to be endured (in Purgatory), except it be lightened by Masses, works of Charity, Pilgrimages, Fasts, and such like; or else shortened by pardon for term or by Plenary pardon quite removed and taken away. This is the mystery of the Man of sin. This maze the Church of Rome doth cause her followers to tread when they ask her the way to Justification. I cannot stand now to unrip this building, and sift it piece by piece; only I will pass it by in few words, that that may befall Babylon, in the presence of that which God hath builded, as happened unto Dagon before the Ark."

Richard Hooker

Richard Hooker continues, (p.502–3) "'Doubtless', (says the Apostle), 'I have counted all things lost, and judged them to be dung that I may win Christ; and to be found in Him, not having my own righteousness, but that which is through the Faith of Christ, the righteousness which is of God through Faith.' (Philippians 3.8–9.) Whether they speak of the first or second Justification, they make the essence of a divine quality inherent, they make it righteousness which is in us. If it be in us, then it is ours, as our souls are ours, though we have them from God, and can hold them no longer than pleaseth Him; if He withdraw the breath of our nostrils, we fall to dust: but the righteousness wherein we must be found, if we will be justified, is not our own; therefore we cannot be justified by any inherent quality. Christ hath merited righteousness for as many as are found in Him. In Him God findeth us, if we be faithful; for by Faith we are incorporated into Christ. Then, although in ourselves we be altogether sinful and unrighteous, yet even the man which is impious in himself, full of iniquity, full of sin; him being found in Christ through Faith, and having his sin remitted through repentance; him God beholdeth with a gracious eye, putting away his sin by not imputing it, taketh quite away the punishment due thereto by pardoning it, and accepteth him in Jesus Christ as perfectly righteousness, as if he had fulfilled all that was commanded in the Law; shall I say more perfectly righteous than if himself had fulfilled the whole Law? I must take heed what I say: but the Apostle saith, 'God made Him to be sin for us, who knew no sin; that we might be made the righteousness of God in Him.' .... You see, therefore, that the Church of Rome in teaching Justification by inherent Grace doth pervert the truth of Christ; and that by the hands of the Apostles we have received otherwise than she teacheth." What could be clearer?

John Owen

John Owen shows throughout the Old Testament in the antithesis of "Condemning the Wicked" and "Justifying the Righteous" (I Kings 8.31-32. Isaiah 50.8. etc.) that to condemn never means to make wicked or infuse wickedness into any, but only to pronounce wicked or unjust, and to justify, equally means to pronounce just or righteous, and not to infuse righteousness or to make just. As regards the Greek word for Justification in the New Testament, Owen shows (Works. Vol.XI. p.160-161) in every use of the Greek verb "dikaioun", excepting four cases, it can be clearly shown, only to mean "to pronounce" or "declare righteous." In three places where there is any possible uncertainty (Romans 8.30. I Cor.6. 11. and Titus 3.5-7.) to "impart righteousness" cannot be conclusively established as the sole meaning, and it is still in the context able to bear the meaning "to pronounce righteous." Only in one case (Rev.22.11.) is there a doubt. Owen says that, "There are few Protestants who do not acknowledge that the word cannot be here used in a forensic sense (to pronounce righteous), but that 'to be justified' in Rev.22.11. is to go on and increase in piety and righteousness." (Works. Vol.XI. p.166). He adds, "No more can be intended, but that he who is righteous, should so proceed in working righteousness, as to secure his justified estate unto himself, and to manifest it before God and the world." (Works. Vol.XI. p.167). This is in keeping with the use of similar expressions by John the Divine in his 1st Epistle 2.29. where he speaks of "Everyone that doeth righteousness," and in Ch.3.7. of the same Epistle where again he says, "He that doeth righteousness is righteous." John Owen confirms that out of 36 uses of the word concerning Justification in the New Testament, the only real doubt as to the clear meaning "to acquit or pronounce righteous" occurs in this one place.

The Consensus of the Hebrew and Greek

Putting together the consensus of Hebrew and Greek, the Scriptures show that the original languages sustain one meaning for Justification, namely that God acquits and declares His people righteous in the person and for the sake of His Son. Romans 3.24 shows only one way, "Being justified freely by His grace through the redemption that is in Christ Jesus." There is no support in the Canonical Scriptures for any other meaning or definition of Justification, and if any other is accepted it must be based upon a tradition outside of the Holy Scriptures. To allow anything else, is to give credence to the Roman Catholic claims that the Pope and Church are above Scripture and are its interpreter. An inherent, infused, imparted righteousness is nowhere spoken of in Holy Scripture. Section 15 of the agreed ARCIC statement says, (following the thinking of Cardinal Henry Newman), "His creative word imparts what it imputes. By pronouncing us righteous, God also makes us righteous. He imparts a righteousness which is His and becomes ours." The answer to this is that certainly God is able to speak and it is done. But Scripture shows that God declares and pronounces the sinner righteous in the person of His Son. Nowhere does Scripture speak of Him imparting righteousness. All our righteousnesses are as filthy rags. To stand before the Throne of God in that great day, we must be clothed in the spotless robe of Christ's righteousness. God will be just and the justifier of him that believeth in Jesus. Good works *must* follow – "We are His workmanship created in Christ Jesus unto good works, which God hath before ordained that we should walk in them." (Eph.2.10.) "By their fruits shall ye know them." (Matt.7.20.) But works form no meritorious part of our salvation. Christ is our Saviour – He washes away our sins in His precious blood. (I John 1.7.)

Other Aspects of "Salvation and the Church"

By translating Justification as "to make righteous", Roman Catholic theologians have identified it with sanctification and in this way have woven a web of confusion which appears in Section 15 of the agreed statement. Protestants will be repelled by the pronouncement of the agreed statement in Section 16 that "Baptism is the unrepeatable sacrament of Justification." How has infant sprinkling, a Protestant may well ask, anything to do with Justification? "Being justified by Faith, we have peace with God through our Lord Jesus Christ." (Romans 5.1.) The answer to the question is that Roman Catholics believe in baptismal regeneration – that is that divine Grace is given to an infant at the moment of baptism. Infant sprinkling rather than being a sign, is a sacramental infusion of Grace and is described in Section 12 of the statement as, "Baptism, the sacrament of Faith." From this basis, the Church of Rome pleads for a double justification. The first, consisting in the remission of sin and the renovation of the inward man, is said to be by Faith, in a sense however, which does not exclude merit and pre-disposing qualifications; the second, whereby we are adjudged to everlasting life, is said to be by inherent righteousness and by works, performed by the aid of that Grace which was infused in the first. Concil. Trident., SESS., vi., de Justificatione. (The Reformed Faith. Robert Shaw. p.126.) The mass is described in the statement (Sec.16) – "The Eucharist is the repeated Sacrament by which the life of Christ's body is constituted and renewed when the death of Christ is proclaimed until He comes again." Such masses are said to be a means of grace in and of themselves, not only for the living but for the dead.

Similarities between ARCIC II and the Diet of Ratisbon 1541.

We may justifiably ask what Martin Luther's reaction to ARCIC II might have been. He was no stranger to attempts to conflate the Reformation doctrine of Justification by Faith alone in the finished work of Christ with the Roman Catholic interpretation. At the Diet of Ratisbon (1541), this blending had almost been achieved, until the precise function of the Faith by which we are justified was examined. "According to the Protestant doctrine, it is the means of justification simply because it receives and rests upon Christ alone..... According to the Roman Catholic doctrine, Faith justifies, not by uniting the sinner to Christ and making him a partaker of Christ's righteousness, but by 'working' in him, and 'sanctifying' him – by being in its own essential nature as one of the 'fruits of the Spirit' and by producing in its actual operation as a vital principle which 'worketh by love' a real inherent righteousness, which is, on its own account, acceptable to God, and which constitutes the immediate ground of his acceptance, in short by making him righteous." (Justification. James Buchanan. p.146–7.) Thus the Roman Catholic theologians accepted Justification by Faith in Jesus Christ at Ratisbon but in all their concessions reserved one point carefully expressed in ambiguous terms. Buchanan goes on to say, "There can be no honest compromise between the Popish and Protestant doctrine of Justification – the one is at direct variance with the other, not in respect of verbal expression merely, but in respect of their fundamental principles, – and any settlement, on the basis of mutual concession, could only be made by means of ambiguous expressions, and could amount to nothing more than a hollow truce, liable to be broken by either party as soon as the subject was brought again into serious discussion. This was the abortive result of the apparent agreement at Ratisbon; it settled no question, it satisfied no party, and it led afterwards to much misunderstanding and mutual recrimination. 'Let them go on,' said Luther, referring to the schemes of those who thought that the differences between Roman Catholics and Protestants might be made up by such conferences, 'We shall not envy the success of their labours: they will be the first who could ever convert the devil and reconcile him to Christ..... The sceptre of the Lord admits of no bending and joining; but must remain straight and unchanged, the rule of Faith and practice.' The double policy of the Roman Church so strikingly exhibited at Ratisbon, in first rejecting the Protestant doctrine of Justification as an unauthorised and dangerous 'novelty', and afterwards claiming it in their own sense, as a truth which they had always taught and held, was pursued in several successive Diets of the Empire." (p.151–2). The same error at the Council of Trent is exhibited in its Canons and Decrees in Chapter XVI, Canon IX; "If anyone saith, that by Faith alone the impious is justified in such wise as to mean, that nothing else is required to co-operate in order to the obtaining of the Grace of Justification, and that it is not in any way necessary, that he be prepared and disposed by the movement of his own will: let him be anathema." And in Canon XXIV, "If anyone saith, that the justice received is not preserved and also increased before God through good works; but that the said works are merely the fruits and signs of Justification obtained but not a cause of the increase thereof: let him be anathema."

The Ambiguities of ARCIC II

The agreed statement is not as concise as Canon IX and XXIV, but neither does the statement utterly reject the two Canons. There are undoubted concessions toward the Reformation doctrine of Justification and so in Section 30 we read, "Of those who are justified by Grace," and again in Section 18 we read, "The term Justification speaks of a divine declaration of acquittal." But equally Section 17 demonstrates the attempt to blend the Catholic and the Protestant doctrines in the words, "Thus the righteousness of God our Saviour is not only declared in a judgement made by God in favour of sinners, but it is also bestowed as a gift to make them righteous." Here inherent righteousness, which Richard Hooker describes as "a perversion of the truth," is conflated with imputed righteousness. Section 18 contains the expression, "Christ's perfect righteousness is reckoned to our account." This is sound Protestant doctrine, but it is followed at once in Section 19 by a description of "good works," which are described as "truly good," and later we are told, "God involves us in what He freely does to realise our salvation," and then follows a quotation from St. Augustine, "The God who made you without you, without you, does not make you just." All this leads towards some place for works in Justification. Certain Scriptures are conspicuously absent such as, "To him that worketh not, but believeth on Him that justifieth the ungodly, his faith is counted for righteousness. Even as David also describeth the blessedness of the man under whom God imputeth righteousness without works." (Romans 4,5–6.) Again Ephesians 2,8–9. is noteworthy for its absence, "By grace are ye saved, through faith and that not of yourselves it is the gift of God: not of works, lest any man should boast."

Further Aspects of ARCIC II

The ARCIC II document is an obviously Ecumenical document. Holy Scripture has been given equal value with Church Traditions; facets of truth from Protestantism and errors of Catholicism stand side by side. Justification is confused with sanctification. Justification is removed from the clear primacy given it by the Reformers. Termed by Luther, *"Articulus stantis vel cadentis ecclesiae,"* "the test by which the Church stands or falls," it no longer has this place in the ARCIC II statement; in fact sanctification is discussed first in Section 17 and justification follows in Section 18. The statement says, "Thus the juridical aspect of Justification, while expressing an important facet of the truth, is not the exclusive notion in the light of which all other Biblical ideas and images of salvation must be interpreted. For God sanctifies as well as acquits." (Section 18). This is a flat denial of the place given to justification by the Reformers. And so we read, "The works of the righteous performed in Christian freedom and in the love of God which the Holy Spirit gives us are the object of God's commendation and receive their reward." (Section 23). This is far removed from "the just shall live by faith," and "salvation is not of works." Later in Section 23, we read, "This reward is a gift depending wholly on divine Grace." But the foundation of justification is still not resting wholly on the merit of Christ, but includes some of our imperfect works. There is a deep subtilty in the ambiguity of Section 23. In Section 22 the document lets in priestly absolution, the confessional and penances with the words, "The Church is entrusted by the Lord with authority to pronounce forgiveness in His name to those who have fallen into sin and repent. The Church may also help them to a deeper realisation of the mercy of God by asking for practical amends for what has been done amiss." The Mass is enunciated under the language of Section 16, "The Eucharist is the repeated sacrament," and later described in Section 27 as, "This once for all atoning work of Christ realised and experienced in the life of the Church and celebrated in the Eucharist." Celebration here certainly contains more than remembrance. This is true in the light of the Final Report of ARCIC I where the Lord's Supper is described as, "no mere calling to mind as the New Testament says, of a past event or its significance, but rather the making effective in the present of an event in the past," i.e. redemption must still be accomplished daily in the 20th Century on Roman Catholic altars. What is contained in the last clause but one of Section 25 is not difficult to see. "Those who respond in faith to the Gospel come to the way of salvation through incorporation by baptism into the Church." If "the Church" is the Church of Rome under the Pope (as we believe the word Church must mean throughout the Reports of ARCIC I and II) then it is clear that Christians are only those who are made members of that Church by baptism.

Conclusions

It appears in examining ARCIC I and II agreed statements, that the Church of Rome is preserved relatively intact. The Anglicans appear to be about to sacrifice Article 6 of the Thirty Nine Articles to concede a place for Tradition alongside Holy Scripture. The ARCIC II document refers to "ideas and images of salvation" as opposed to Scripturally inspired truths. The door is wide open for the Mass to remain. The Confessional, priestly absolution and penance are all here. Baptismal regeneration is the method of "incorporation into the believing community." The Anglican Service for baptism of infants is exceptionally weak at this point and leaves this door wide open. One word characterises this document, "Salvation and the Church," and that is compromise, and that of a dangerously subtle nature. But it is encouraging that there are a few in the Anglican Church and outside of it, who are willing to rise to the defence of the historic Protestant commitment of our National Church. Christian division is a "scandal" as ARCIC II says. But we deny that "through baptism we are united to Christ." (Section 1.) The Scriptures say of baptism, "*Not* the putting away of the filth of the flesh, but the answer of a good conscience toward God," 1 Peter 3.21, and add, "Ye must be born again." John 3.7. We deny that "the community of believers, united with Christ, gives praise and thanksgiving to God, *celebrating* the Grace of Christ as they await His return in glory," (Section 1.) for we see here nothing less than the priest celebrating the Mass as the Pope has constantly done in stadiums around the world in recent years.

Final Questions

The final questions remain. Do Indulgences stay in the Roman Catholic Church? The Reformation commenced over Luther's attack on Indulgences. Is Purgatory to remain or shall the truth be affirmed of the apostle Paul, "Absent from the body, present with the Lord." What about Requiem Masses and prayers for the dead? Is the Confessional and priestly absolution to remain? What about the worship of the Virgin Mary? Is the invocation of Saints still to be a practice of the Roman Catholic Church? The Pope has several times in recent years been to the shrines of the Virgin Mary and prostrated himself before the images of the Virgin, who is variously described as co-redeemer with Christ. Protestants reaffirm what Luther affirmed in his day regarding the truths of the Reformation, "Here I stand, so help me God." "Salvation and the Church" is a cloudy, misty document containing a strange blend of truth and error, so subtle that it is difficult to unravel. One thing is abundantly clear – it lacks entirely the Scriptural ring of "the Westminster Confession of Faith" and its articles on Justification. It is a major departure from the Homilies of Cranmer and the Thirty Nine Articles of Faith. May there yet rise in this country the authentic voice of Scripture, as it rose in the days of the Reformers, the Puritans and the 18th Century Evangelicals.

James Buchanan – A Final Word

James Buchanan, Professor of Systematic Theology at New College, Edinburgh wrote in his masterly survey on "Justification" (p.232–3) in 1867, "About 1840, there sprang up rival schools at Oxford – the one represented by the 'Tracts for the Times,' and tending towards Romanism – the other by the 'Essays and Reviews,' and strongly tinctured with rationalism. Looking at the progress which these two systems have already made and the actual state of religious opinion in this country at the present day, who will venture to say what will be the prevailing theology of our grand-children. God may be pleased once more to pour out His Spirit on the Churches, and to raise up, perhaps from the poorest of His people, a band of humble, but devoted, believers, men of faith and prayer, as 'living epistles of Christ known and read of all men,' the noblest witnesses of Christ in the land. What we most need is a great spiritual revival, which, commencing in the hearts of our congregations, will work from within outwards, and from beneath upwards, destroying 'the wisdom of the wise, and bringing to nought the understanding of the prudent,' and making it manifest to all that the Gospel is still 'mighty through God to the pulling down of strongholds.' Our immediate prospects are dark and threatening; and 'men's hearts are beginning to fail them for fear, and for looking after those things which are coming on the earth.' What course events may take it is impossible to foretell; but, looking to mere human probability, of two schemes, one or other is likely to be attempted, or perhaps each of them in succession; either the Established Churches will be stript of a definite creed, if not by a legislative act, by the more insidious method of judge-made law; and made so comprehensive as to include men of all shades of opinion, from semi-Popery, through the various grades of Pelagian, Arian, and Socinian error, down to ill-disguised infidelity; or, if the moral sense of the community revolts from the indiscriminate support of truth and error, then, the entire disestablishment of the Church in these islands, perhaps till the time when 'all the kingdoms of this world shall become the kingdoms of our God, and of His Christ.' Of the Church of Christ there is no fear: she is 'founded on a rock, and the gates of hell shall not prevail against her.' Somewhere in the earth she will find an asylum, should it be only as 'the woman flying into the wilderness:' but for any particular Church, or any particular country, there is no absolute security, that her 'candlestick will not be removed out of its place, except she repents'. Let us pray that 'when the enemy is coming in like a flood, the Spirit of the

Lord may lift up a standard against him;' and that those young men who are about to enter on the ministry 'in troublous times,' may have a banner given to them, 'that it may be displayed because of the truth' – a banner bearing this inspired inscription: **'I am not ashamed of the Gospel of Christ: for it is the power of God unto salvation to everyone that believeth;..... for therein is the righteousness of God revealed from faith to faith, as it is written, The just shall live by faith'**. (Romans 1.16–17)."

Recommended Reading
Thirty Nine Articles of the Church of England
Homilies of the Church of England: No.3 "Of Salvation" – Thomas Cranmer
Westminster Confession of Faith
The Confession of Faith – A.A. Hodge
The Reformed Faith – Robert Shaw
The Savoy Declaration: 1658
"Things Most Surely Believed Among Us." (The 1689 Baptist Confession of Faith)
The Doctrine of Justification – James Buchanan
Historical Theology – William Cunningham
Justification – John Owen (Works, Vol.XI)
Commentary on Romans (Appendix A 'Justification.') – Prof. John Murray
Systematic Theology (Chapter 17 'Justification') – Prof. John Murray (Collected Writings. Vol.II.)

HD   Kay, Geoffrey
4901   The economic ~~history~~ *theory* of
K36   the working class
1979

DATE DUE			

DEMCO